Student Edition

A Firm
Foundation

Building a Household of Faith on the Unchanging
Principles of the Word of God

PAUL CHAPPELL

First published in 2005 by Striving Together Publications, a ministry of Lancaster Baptist Church, Lancaster, CA 93535. Striving Together Publications is committed to providing tried, trusted, and proven books that will further equip local churches to carry out the Great Commission. Your comments and suggestions are valued.

Striving Together Publications
4020 E. Lancaster Blvd.
Lancaster, CA 93535
800.201.7748

Cover design by Daniel Irmler
Layout by Craig Parker
Edited by Robert Byers, Cary Schmidt, Amanda Michael, and Esther Brown

ISBN 0-9652859-8-7

Printed in the United States of America

Table of Contents

Faith in God's Plan for Your Marriage

Key Verses

"And the Lord God caused a deep sleep to fall upon Adam, and he slept: and he took one of his ribs, and closed up the flesh instead thereof; And the rib, which the Lord God had taken from man, made he a woman, and brought her unto the man. And Adam said, This is now bone of my bones, and flesh of my flesh: she shall be called Woman, because she was taken out of Man. Therefore shall a man leave his father and his mother, and shall cleave unto his wife: and they shall be one flesh. And they were both naked, the man and his wife, and were not ashamed."—Genesis 2:21-25

Overview

In this passage we see principles that define God's idea of what marriage should be like. God has a plan for your marriage. He knows what will work to bring Him honor and glory. You need to determine that you will learn and follow that plan in faith for your marriage to reach God's ultimate design.

Introduction

_____

_____

_____

I. The _____ of Marriage

"It is not good that the man should be alone."—GENESIS 2:18

A. _____

"Whoso findeth a wife findeth a good thing, and obtaineth favour of the Lord."—PROVERBS 18:22

B. _____

"There was not found an help meet for him."
—GENESIS 2:20

II. The _____ about Marriage

"This is now bone of my bones, and flesh of my flesh."
—GENESIS 2:23

A. A Proclamation of _____

B. A Proclamation of _____

"Likewise, ye husbands, dwell with them according to knowledge, giving honour unto the wife, as unto the weaker vessel, and as being heirs together of the grace of life; that your prayers be not hindered."—1 PETER 3:7

III. The _____ of Marriage

A. _____

B. _____

"For this cause shall a man leave his father and mother, and cleave to his wife; And they twain shall be one flesh: so then they are no more twain, but one flesh. What therefore God hath joined together, let not man put asunder."—MARK 10:7–9

C. _____

    1. WEAVING _____

    2. WEAVING _____

    3. WEAVING _____

Conclusion

_____

_____

_____

Study Questions

1. Why do many families turn anywhere but to God for advice about marriage?

2. What two vital things is marriage designed to provide?

3. List three convictions that must remain priorities in your marriage.

4. What is one of the most important foundations of marriage?

5. Why should you have faith in God's plan for your marriage?

6. How has your acceptance of your spouse changed since you were first married? What adjustments should be made?

7. What are some ways you can outwardly honor each other?

8. List some suggestions for growing together spiritually, emotionally, and physically. What can you do today to start applying these things?

Memory Verse

MARK 10:7–9—*"For this cause shall a man leave his father and mother, and cleave to his wife; And they twain shall be one flesh: so then they are no more twain, but one flesh. What therefore God hath joined together, let not man put asunder."*

Developing Oneness in Your Marriage

Key Verses

"And the Lord God caused a deep sleep to fall upon Adam, and he slept: and he took one of his ribs, and closed up the flesh instead thereof; And the rib, which the Lord God had taken from man, made he a woman, and brought her unto the man. And Adam said, This is now bone of my bones, and flesh of my flesh: she shall be called Woman, because she was taken out of Man. Therefore shall a man leave his father and his mother, and shall cleave unto his wife: and they shall be one flesh. And they were both naked, the man and his wife, and were not ashamed."—GENESIS 2:21–25

Overview

It seems like real oneness and unity are elusive goals for a lot of people. Even many people who are committed Christians struggle with developing true intimacy in their relationships. Society accepts that there should be tension and disharmony in marriage. Today, we find that many Christians settle for an uneasy truce. But that is not God's plan. He wants your marriage to be a relationship of blessing and harmony.

Introduction

_____

_____

_____

I. A Commitment to Permanence

A. *Through Complete* Acceptance

* cannot be conditional or performance based

B. *Through Complete* Commitment

"Therefore shall a man leave his father and his mother, and shall cleave unto his wife: and they shall be one flesh."—Genesis 2:24

1. MAKE A COMMITMENT TO purposeful LIVING
"For this cause shall a man leave his father and mother, and cleave to his wife."—Mark 10:7

2. MAKE A COMMITMENT TO Biblical PRINCIPLES

* commitment to God, children, + spouse

II. A Commitment to Spiritual Unity

A. *Our Highest* Example *of Unity*

1. THE Father EXALTS THE Son
"God, who at sundry times and in divers manners spake in time past unto the fathers by the prophets, Hath in these last days spoken unto us by his Son,

whom he hath appointed heir of all things, by whom also he made the worlds; But unto the Son he saith, Thy throne, O God, is for ever and ever: a sceptre of righteousness is the sceptre of thy kingdom."
—HEBREWS 1:1–2, 8

2. THE **Son** EXALTS THE **Father**

"Jesus saith unto them, My meat is to do the will of him that sent me, and to finish his work."
—JOHN 4:34

"I have glorified thee on the earth: I have finished the work which thou gavest me to do."
—JOHN 17:4

3. THE **Spirt** EXALTS THE **Son**

"Howbeit when he, the Spirit of truth, is come, he will guide you into all truth: for he shall not speak of himself; but whatsoever he shall hear, that shall he speak: and he will shew you things to come. He shall glorify me: for he shall receive of mine, and shall shew it unto you."—JOHN 16:13–14

B. Our Highest **Hope** for Unity

1. YOU MUST KNOW CHRIST AS **Savior**

2. YOU MUST ACKNOWLEDGE CHRIST AS **Lord**
"Ye call me Master and Lord: and ye say well; for so I am."—JOHN 13:13

III. A Commitment to _Openness_

A. _Hindrance_ to Openness

1. _Selfishness_

"*Let nothing be done through strife or vainglory; but in lowliness of mind let each esteem other better than themselves.*" —PHILIPPIANS 2:3

2. _Insecurity_

3. _Competition_

4. _____ _____ AND EXPECTATIONS

B. _____ to Openness

1. _____

2. _____

3. _____

Conclusion

_____

_____

_____

Study Questions

1. To develop oneness in marriage, what three commitments should you make to/with your spouse?

2. What two things are essential for permanence in marriage?

3. What is the best way to be a good husband/wife?

4. The Devil knows that if he can destroy openness, he can destroy your intimacy. What four things does he use to hinder openness in a relationship?

5. List some things you can do in the next week, month, and year that will demonstrate your commitment to your spouse.

6. Compare and contrast the relationship between you and your spouse to the relationship of the Trinity.

7. How can you fight the Devil's attacks on openness in your marriage?

8. Accepting, yielding to, and appreciating your spouse encourages openness in your relationship. In which attitude(s) do you need to grow the most? What will you do to see growth?

Memory Verse

EPHESIANS 5:28–29—*"So ought men to love their wives as their own bodies. He that loveth his wife loveth himself. For no man ever yet hated his own flesh; but nourisheth and cherisheth it, even as the Lord the church:"*

How To Have a Truly Christian Home

Key Verses

"And the Lord God said, It is not good that the man should be alone: I will make him an help meet for him. And the Lord God caused a deep sleep to fall upon Adam and he slept: and he took one of his ribs, and closed up the flesh instead thereof; And the rib, which the Lord God had taken from man, made he a woman, and brought her unto the man. And Adam said, This is now bone of my bones, and flesh of my flesh: she shall be called Woman, because she was taken out of Man. Therefore shall a man leave his father and his mother, and shall cleave unto his wife: and they shall be one flesh." —GENESIS 2:18, 21-24

Overview

From the very beginning of human history, the family has been the basic building block of society. God instituted the family as part of His plan for the people He had created. The home is to be a place where God's love is modeled and the next generation is mentored in their faith. The only way to have a true Christian home is by following the guidelines of God's Word.

Introduction

_____

_____

_____

I. _____ **through Jesus Christ**

A. *Parents Must Teach the* _____ *of Christ*

"When I call to remembrance the unfeigned faith that
is in thee, which dwelt first in thy grandmother Lois,
and thy mother Eunice; and I am persuaded that in thee
also."—2 TIMOTHY 1:5

B. *Salvation Is a Personal* _____

"And that from a child thou hast known the holy
scriptures, which are able to make thee wise unto
salvation through faith which is in Christ Jesus."
—2 TIMOTHY 3:15

"So then faith cometh by hearing, and hearing by the
word of God."—ROMANS 10:17

II. _____ **to the Holy Spirit**

A. *Surrender Produces an Attitude of* _____

"Speaking to yourselves in psalms and hymns and
spiritual songs, singing and making melody in your heart
to the Lord."—EPHESIANS 5:19

"Let the word of Christ dwell in you richly in all wisdom; teaching and admonishing one another in psalms and hymns and spiritual songs, singing with grace in your hearts to the Lord."—COLOSSIANS 3:16

B. Surrender Produces an Attitude of _____ _

"Giving thanks always for all things unto God and the Father in the name of our Lord Jesus Christ."
—EPHESIANS 5:20

C. Surrender Produces an Attitude of _____

"Submitting yourselves one to another in the fear of God."—EPHESIANS 5:21

For rebellion is as the sin of witchcraft, and stubbornness is as iniquity and idolatry. Because thou hast rejected the word of the Lord, he hath also rejected thee from being king."—1 SAMUEL 15:23

III. _____ through Biblical Order

A. Husbands Are To Provide _____

B. Wives Are To _____ Their Husbands' Leadership

"Wives, submit yourselves unto your own husbands, as unto the Lord."—EPHESIANS 5:22

C. Children Are To _____ Their Parents
"My son, give me thine heart, and let thine eyes observe my ways."—PROVERBS 23:26

IV. _____ through Godly Living

A. Through _____ on the Word of God
"Sanctify them through thy truth: thy word is truth."
—JOHN 17:17

B. Through _____ _____

Conclusion

_____

_____

_____

Study Questions

1. What are the four requirements for having a truly Christian home?

2. What is the most important job you have as a parent?

3. What role should the husband take in the family? the wife? the children?

4. Sanctification comes through _____.

5. List three attitudes of a family surrendered to the Holy Spirit. Which of these attitudes is most prevalent in your family? Which is least prevalent?

6.   Leadership is not domination; it is service. What kind of leader are you?

7.   Can you say to your children, "I want you to follow the way that I live"? Are there areas in your life that you would not want them to follow?

8.   Is the Word of God the center and focus of your home? List several ways the Word of God can be used in the home to promote sanctification.

Memory Verse

ROMANS 8:8–9—*"So then they that are in the flesh cannot please God. But ye are not in the flesh, but in the Spirit, if so be that the Spirit of God dwell in you. Now if any man have not the Spirit of Christ, he is none of his."*

Healing a Hurting Home

Key Verses

"Likewise, ye wives, be in subjection to your own husbands; that, if any obey not the word, they also may without the word be won by the conversation of the wives; While they behold your chaste conversation, coupled with fear. Whose adorning let it not be that outward adorning of plaiting the hair, and of wearing gold, or of putting on of apparel; But let it be the hidden man of the heart, in that which is not corruptible, even the ornament of a meek and quiet spirit, which is in the sight of God of great price. For after this manner in the old time the holy women also, who trusted in God, adorned themselves, being in subjection unto their own husbands: Even as Sara obeyed Abraham, calling him lord: whose daughter ye are, as long as ye do well, and are not afraid with any amazement. Likewise, ye husbands, dwell with them according to knowledge, giving honour unto the wife, as unto the weaker vessel, and as being heirs together of the grace of life; that your prayers be not hindered."
—1 PETER 3:1–7

Overview

Many marriages are crumbling today. God is the Great Physician, and He has a remedy that can cure any problem in your marriage. We must be willing to learn and to follow His "prescription" for a hurting home to be truly healed.

Introduction

_____

_____

_____

I. Living _____

"Likewise, ye wives, be in subjection to your own husbands; that, if any obey not the word, they also may without the word be won by the conversation of the wives."—1 PETER 3:1

"Humble yourselves in the sight of the Lord, and he shall lift you up."—JAMES 4:10

A. *Before* _____

B. *Before* _____ _____
"Only by pride cometh contention: but with the well advised is wisdom."—PROVERBS 13:10

II. Living _____

"While they behold your chaste conversation, coupled with fear." —1 PETER 3:2

A. *A Helpful Wife Is a* _____ *Wife*

B. *A Helpful Husband Is a* _____-_____ *Husband*

III. Living _____

A. Dwelling with _____

    1. ASK GOD FOR _____

    2. _____

B. Dwelling with _____

    1. WITH OUR _____
"And whatsoever ye do in word or deed, do all in the name of the Lord Jesus, giving thanks to God and the Father by him."—COLOSSIANS 3:17

    2. WITH OUR _____
"Let your speech be alway with grace, seasoned with salt, that ye may know how ye ought to answer every man."—COLOSSIANS 4:6

Conclusion

_____

_____

_____

Study Questions

1. What does it take to heal a hurting home?

2. The beginning of humility in the home is _____.

3. How can a husband/wife live helpfully?

4. To honor your spouse, you must dwell with what two things?

5. Pride is the antithesis of humility. What are some ways to reconcile the damage of pride in your marriage?

6. What is the difference between a thermometer and a thermostat? Which one are you?

7. When was the last time you really listened to your spouse? How can you improve your listening skills?

8. Are you in the habit of using kind words or hurtful words?

Memory Verse

1 PETER 3:8—*"Finally, be ye all of one mind, having compassion one of another, love as brethren, be pitiful, be courteous:"*

Developing the Heart of Your Child

Key Verses

"But Daniel purposed in his heart that he would not defile himself with the portion of the king's meat, nor with the wine which he drank: therefore he requested of the prince of the eunuchs that he might not defile himself."—DANIEL 1:8

"Shadrach, Meshach, and Abednego, answered and said to the king, O Nebuchadnezzar, we are not careful to answer thee in this matter. If it be so, our God whom we serve is able to deliver us from the burning fiery furnace, and he will deliver us out of thine hand, O king. But if not, be it known unto thee, O king, that we will not serve thy gods, nor worship the golden image which thou hast set up."
—DANIEL 3:16–18

Overview

As parents we have an opportunity while our children are young to set them on a course for a lifetime of service to God. The key to helping them overcome the pressures of the world is to develop in their lives a heart for God. The heart determines the decisions of life, and there are specific things parents can do to cultivate a right heart attitude toward God in their children.

Introduction

_____

_____

_____

I. We Must Develop a _____ Heart

A. *Purpose Begins at* _____

B. *Purpose Is* _____ *through the Word of God*

"He taught me also, and said unto me, Let thine heart retain my words: keep my commandments, and live."
—Proverbs 4:4

II. We Must Develop a _____ Heart

A. *A* _____ *Heart Leads to* _____ *Living*

"Seeing ye have purified your souls in obeying the truth through the Spirit unto unfeigned love of the brethren, see that ye love one another with a pure heart fervently."—1 PETER 1:22

"Blessed are the pure in heart: for they shall see God."
—MATTHEW 5:8

"Sanctify them through thy truth: thy word is truth."
—JOHN 17:17

*"My God hath sent his angel, and hath shut the lions'
mouths, that they have not hurt me: forasmuch as before
him innocency was found in me; and also before thee, O
king, have I done no hurt."*—DANIEL 6:22

B. A _____ *Heart Leads to* _____ *Living*
*"Unto the pure all things are pure: but unto them that
are defiled and unbelieving is nothing pure; but even
their mind and conscience is defiled."*—TITUS 1:15

III. We Must Develop a _____ Heart

A. _____ *Principles from God's Word*
"Be ye therefore followers of God, as dear children"
— EPHESIANS 5:1

B. _____ *Principles in Your Family Life*

Conclusion

_____

_____

_____

Study Questions

1. What kind of heart should you strive to develop in your children?

2. When should you begin teaching your children God's Word?

3. A pure heart results in what kind of a relationship with God?

4. Where can children learn godly principles?

5. Children value what their parents value. How can you model the importance of Scripture in your life?

6. What can you do to nurture your child to develop a pure heart and protect him from a defiled heart?

7. Are your children's lives and actions dictated by obedience or convenience?

8. Is your heart pure, purposeful, and principled? Do your children see it?

Memory Verse

JOHN 17:17—*"Sanctify them through thy truth: thy word is truth."*

A Biblical View of the Family

Key Verses

"And the Lord God said, It is not good that the man should be alone; I will make him an help meet for him. And the Lord God caused a deep sleep to fall upon Adam, and he slept: and he took one of his ribs, and closed up the flesh instead thereof; And the rib, which the Lord God had taken from man, made he a woman, and brought her unto the man."—GENESIS 2:18, 21–22

Overview

Marriage as an institution in our country is in trouble. And the crumbling of the American family is having a devastating effect on our society and culture. Despite the trends around us, we can still build strong families that survive the storms by going back to God's original design for the family.

Introduction

_____

_____

_____

I. God's _____ for the Family

    A. The Family Provides _____

    B. The Family Provides _____

    C. The Family Provides _____

       1. FAMILY _____

       2. FAMILY _____

II. The World's _____ from God's Design

III. The _____ of Strong Families

    A. Follow Biblical _____ *for Marriage*

1. **CHRIST-LIKE** _____
*"Husbands, love your wives, even as Christ also
loved the church, and gave himself for it."*
—EPHESIANS 5:25

2. **GODLY** _____

B. Teach _____ to Your Children

C. Fathers Accept Their _____
*"And, ye fathers, provoke not your children to wrath:
but bring them up in the nurture and admonition of the
Lord."*—EPHESIANS 6:4

Conclusion

_____

_____

_____

Study Questions

1. What is the source of the greatest problems in our society?

2. The family is to provide what three things?

3. In light of the world's departure from God's design, what do your children need to see?

4. What is Christ-like love?

5. Husband/wife, are you providing the companionship and completion that meets the other's needs? Are there things you need to honestly talk through to make your relationship better?

6. Have you made a decision to have a strong, God-honoring family?

7. Are you teaching your children about God's plan for marriage, or are you letting the world do it?

8. Dad, do you say "I love you" and "I'm sorry" in the home?

Memory Verse

GENESIS 2:24—*"Therefore shall a man leave his father and his mother, and shall cleave unto his wife: and they shall be one flesh."*

The "Three Rs" of a Spirit-Led Family

Key Verses

"And Judah said, The strength of the bearers of burdens is decayed, and there is much rubbish; so that we are not able to build the wall. And our adversaries said, They shall not know, neither see, till we come in the midst among them, and slay them, and cause the work to cease. And it came to pass, that when the Jews which dwelt by them came, they said unto us ten times, From all places whence ye shall return unto us they will be upon you. Therefore set I in the lower places behind the wall, and on the higher places, I even set the people after their families with their swords, their spears, and their bows. And I looked, and rose up, and said unto the nobles, and to the rulers, and to the rest of the people, Be not ye afraid of them: remember the Lord, which is great and terrible, and fight for your brethren, your sons, and your daughters, your wives, and your houses."
—NEHEMIAH 4:10–14

Overview

In no arena do we need God's direction more than in the arena of the Christian family. The Holy Spirit offers direction and leadership to each member of the family through the Word of God to help them learn their roles and fulfill their responsibilities. Doing so helps us have the kind of family life God wants us to enjoy.

Introduction

_____

_____

_____

I. Foundational _____

A. *Parents Are To Fill the Role of a Godly*

_____

B. *Parents Are To Fill the Role of a Godly*

_____

"...follow me, and I will make you fishers of men"
—MATTHEW 4:19

II. Fulfill _____

A. *We Are To* _____ *Our Children*

"My son, give me thine heart, and let thine eyes observe my ways."—PROVERBS 23:26

"The rod and reproof give wisdom: but a child left to himself bringeth his mother to shame."—PROVERBS 29:15

"The wicked are estranged from the womb: they go astray as soon as they be born, speaking lies."
—PSALM 58:3

B. *We Are To* _____ *Our Children*

C. *We Are To* _____ _____ *to*
   Our Children

   1. BEGIN WITH A BIBLE _____

   2. DEVELOP A _____

   3. ESTABLISH A _____

III. Foster _____

A. *Relationships Are Built through* _____
   _____

"Likewise, ye husbands, dwell with them according to knowledge."—1 PETER 3:7

B. *Relationships Are Built through* _____
   _____

Conclusion

_____

_____

_____

Study Questions

1.   What is the definition of a true Christian home?

2.   What are the "three Rs" of a Spirit-led family?

3.   How can you develop standards of protection for your children?

4.   What are the two ways to build a parent/child relationship?

5.   How can your family devotions improve to be more effective for your family?

6.   What do you need to change in your life to be the role model God wants you to be for your children? What are you doing that you do not want them to imitate?

7.   Are you starting to guide your children at a young enough age?

8.   What is the greater influence in your home—you or the television?

Memory Verse

PROVERBS 23:26—"*My son, give me thine heart, and let thine eyes observe my ways.*"

Fight for Your Children

Key Verses

"And Judah said, The strength of the bearers of burdens is decayed, and there is much rubbish; so that we are not able to build the wall. And our adversaries said, They shall not know, neither see, till we come in the midst among them, and slay them, and cause the work to cease. And it came to pass, that when the Jews which dwelt by them came, they said unto us ten times, From all places whence ye shall return unto us they will be upon you. Therefore set I in the lower places behind the wall, and on the higher places, I even set the people after their families with their swords, their spears, and their bows. And I looked, and rose up, and said unto the nobles, and to the rulers, and to the rest of the people, Be not ye afraid of them: remember the Lord, which is great and terrible, and fight for your brethren, your sons, and your daughters, your wives, and your houses."
—NEHEMIAH 4:10–14

Overview

Our children are not growing up in an easy time. Virtually everything in our culture fights against their doing right. If our children are to be the Christians God wants them to be, we as parents must be willing to fight for them. Winning the battle for a child's heart is the key to success as a parent.

Introduction

_____

_____

_____

I. Fight Your _____

_____

    A. _____

    B. _____

    C. _____

II. Fight Your _____

"This I say then, Walk in the Spirit, and ye shall not fulfil the lust of the flesh."—GALATIANS 5:16

    A. _____

    B. _____

    C. _____

III. Fight the _____ in Our Society

A. *Through _____*

B. *Through _____*

C. *Through _____ in the Community*

Conclusion

_____

_____

_____

Study Questions

1. Raising children is more about the _____ than about the _____.

2. List the three "Fs" in fighting your own spiritual battles.

3. What are the four types of parenting styles?

4. In what three ways can you help fight corruption in our society?

5. Will your children change the world, or will the world change your children?

6. Do you allow anger to control your responses to your children? What do you need to work on in the area of anger?

7. When your children hear the word *home*, of what do they think?

8. Are you taking and making time to help dent our world with the Gospel through soulwinning? Do you have a scheduled time for soulwinning every week?

Memory Verse

1 TIMOTHY 4:16—*"Take heed unto thyself, and unto the doctrine; continue in them: for in doing this thou shalt both save thyself, and them that hear thee."*

A Trio of Tools To Strengthen Your Family

Key Verses

"Be not thou envious against evil men, neither desire to be with them. For their heart studieth destruction, and their lips talk of mischief. Through wisdom is an house builded; and by understanding it is established: And by knowledge shall the chambers be filled with all precious and pleasant riches."—PROVERBS 24:1–4

Overview

Our behavior as Christian families should reflect the wisdom God has made available to us through His Word in every area of our lives. The failure of some Christian families does not demonstrate the failure of God's plan; rather it shows our failure to follow that plan as we should.

Introduction

_____

_____

_____

I. The _____ _____ of the Holy Spirit

A. The _____ of the Holy Spirit

"It is the spirit that quickeneth; the flesh profiteth nothing: the words that I speak unto you, they are spirit, and they are life."—JOHN 6:63

B. The _____ of the Holy Spirit

1. HE IS OUR _____

"And I will pray the Father, and he shall give you another Comforter, that he may abide with you for ever."—JOHN 14:16

2. HE IS OUR _____

3. HE _____ JESUS CHRIST

"Howbeit when he, the Spirit of truth, is come, he will guide you into all truth: for he shall not speak of himself; but whatsoever he shall hear, that shall he speak: and he will shew you things to come. He shall

glorify me: for he shall receive of mine, and shall shew it unto you."—JOHN 16:13–14

C. The _____ of the Holy Spirit

1. A _____ LIFESTYLE
"*But the fruit of the Spirit is love, joy, peace, longsuffering, gentleness, goodness, faith, meekness, temperance: against such there is no law.*"
—GALATIANS 5:22–23

2. A ____ _____ LIFESTYLE
"*This I say then, Walk in the Spirit, and ye shall not fulfil the lust of the flesh.*"—GALATIANS 5:16

II. A _____ _____ of Self

A. Pride Is a _____ of Relationships

B. Pride Is _____ by Appropriating Scripture

"*Knowing this, that our old man is crucified with him, that the body of sin might be destroyed, that henceforth we should not serve sin.*"—ROMANS 6:6

"*For in that he died, he died unto sin once: but in that he liveth, he liveth unto God.*"—ROMANS 6:10

III. A _____ _____ of Serving

A. _____ *to One Another*

"Submitting yourselves one to another in the fear of God."—Ephesians 5:21

B. _____ *One Another*

Conclusion

_____

_____

_____

Study Questions

1. When there is a failure, our _____ is faulty
    because God's _____ are always reliable.

2. Everything we ever need is found where?

3. What are the three purposes of the Holy Spirit?

4. List three powerful tools God has provided to build
    and to strengthen your family.

5. When was the last time you allowed the Holy Spirit to
    comfort or to teach you?

6. Is everything in life about YOU? Do your actions show this?

7. List several ways that you can daily practice the principle of submission.

8. When was the last time you consciously set aside your own preferences to serve your spouse or children?

Memory Verse

ROMANS 6:6—*"Knowing this, that our old man is crucified with him, that the body of sin might be destroyed, that henceforth we should not serve sin."*

The Priorities of a Spiritual Family

Key Verses

"Likewise, ye wives, be in subjection to your own husbands; that, if any obey not the word, they also may without the word be won by the conversation of the wives; While they behold your chaste conversation, coupled with fear. Whose adorning let it not be that outward adorning of plaiting the hair, and of wearing gold, or of putting on of apparel; But let it be the hidden man of the heart, in that which is not corruptible, even the ornament of a meek and quiet spirit, which is in the sight of God of great price. For after this manner in the old time the holy women also, who trusted in God, adorned themselves, being in subjection unto their own husbands: Even as Sara obeyed Abraham, calling him lord: whose daughters ye are, as long as ye do well, and are not afraid with any amazement. Likewise, ye husbands, dwell with them according to knowledge, giving honour unto the wife, as unto the weaker vessel, and as being heirs together of the grace of life; that your prayers be not hindered. Finally, be ye all of one mind, having compassion one of another, love as brethren, be pitiful, be courteous: Not rendering evil for evil, or railing for railing: but contrariwise blessing; knowing that ye are thereunto called, that ye should inherit a blessing."—1 PETER 3:1-9

Overview

God's design is that your family will be a strong testimony for righteousness, even as the culture around you collapses into darkness. To survive in this environment, your family must be a spiritual family—a family dedicated to following the leading of the Holy Spirit of God in every area of life.

Introduction

_____

_____

_____

I. The Priority of a _____ _____

A. *The Testimony of a Surrendered* _____

"A soft answer turneth away wrath: but grievous words stir up anger."—PROVERBS 15:1

B. *The Testimony of a Godly* _____

II. The Priority of a _____ _____

A. _____ *Beauty Is Temporary*

"…but though our outward man perish, yet the inward man is renewed day by day."—2 Corinthians 4:16

B. _____ *Beauty Is Eternal*

"Keep thy heart with all diligence; for out of it are the issues of life."—PROVERBS 4:23

III. The Priority of a _____ _____

A. _____

B. _____

"*Husbands, love your wives, and be not bitter against them.*"—COLOSSIANS 3:19

C. _____

D. _____

E. _____

"*Bless them which persecute you: bless, and curse not.*" —ROMANS 12:14

Conclusion

_____

_____

_____

Study Questions

1. What are the priorities of a spiritual family?

2. _____ beauty is temporary while _____ beauty is eternal.

3. Do manners really matter? What is some scriptural evidence?

4. Why should we show forgiveness and pity to others?

5. If you were asked to list your family's priorities, what would be at the top of that list?

6. If you are reading this book as a spouse with an unsaved partner, what is one way God would lead you to improve your testimony in reaching your spouse?

7. If God were to evaluate each member of your family today, would He find that the priority in each life is outward beauty, or is it inward beauty? What is the evidence?

8. On what manners does your family need to work, both practically and spiritually?

Memory Verse

1 SAMUEL 16:7— *"But the LORD said unto Samuel, Look not on his countenance, or on the height of his stature; because I have refused him: for the LORD seeth not as man seeth; for man looketh on the outward appearance, but the LORD looketh on the heart."*

Portrait of a Loving Family

Key Verses

"Submitting yourselves one to another in the fear of God. Wives, submit yourselves unto your own husbands, as unto the Lord. For the husband is the head of the wife, even as Christ is the head of the church: and he is the saviour of the body. Therefore as the church is subject unto Christ, so let the wives be to their own husbands in every thing. Husbands, love your wives, even as Christ also loved the church, and gave himself for it; That he might sanctify and cleanse it with the washing of water by the word, That he might present it to himself a glorious church, not having spot, or wrinkle, or any such thing; but that it should be holy and without blemish. So ought men to love their wives as their own bodies. He that loveth his wife loveth himself. For no man ever yet hated his own flesh; but nourisheth and cherisheth it, even as the Lord the church: For we are members of his body, of his flesh, and of his bones. For this cause shall a man leave his father and mother, and shall be joined unto his wife, and they two shall be one flesh."
—EPHESIANS 5:21–31

Overview

Just as families have their pictures taken together, your family has a spiritual portrait that God sees. His plan for your family is that it will be a picture of His grace. As we reflect the grace of God in our relationships, our homes will be places of love and peace rather than fighting and conflict.

Introduction

_____

_____

_____

I. A Picture of _____

A. *Surrender to the Lord's* _____

B. *Surrender to the Lord's* _____

II. A Picture of _____

A. *Through* _____

1. SET APART TIME FOR _____ BUILDING

2. MAKE GOD'S WORD YOUR _____

3. AGREE ON THE _____
"*But put ye on the Lord Jesus Christ, and make not provision for the flesh, to fulfil the lusts thereof.*"
—ROMANS 13:14

"*I will set no wicked thing before mine eyes: I hate the work of them that turn aside; it shall not cleave to me.*"—PSALM 101:3

B. *Through* _____

1. **CLEANSING THROUGH THE** _____ **OF GOD**

"Thy word have I hid in mine heart, that I might not sin against thee."—PSALM 119:11

"Sanctify them through thy truth: thy word is truth."—JOHN 17:17

2. **CLEANSING THROUGH** _____

"If we confess our sins, he is faithful and just to forgive us our sins, and to cleanse us from all unrighteousness."—1 JOHN 1:9

III. A Picture of _____

A. Jesus _____ *Salvation*

"Neither is there salvation in any other: for there is none other name under heaven given among men, whereby we must be saved."—ACTS 4:12

"Herein is love, not that we loved God, but that he loved us, and sent his Son to be the propitiation for our sins."—1 JOHN 4:10

B. Jesus _____ *Salvation*

"But God commendeth his love toward us, in that, while we were yet sinners, Christ died for us."—ROMANS 5:8

Conclusion

_____

_____

_____

Study Questions

1. What is the definition of submission?

2. What are three actions that provide protection in the home?

3. What are the two cleansing agents God has provided?

4. What Scripture passage illustrates God's plan of salvation?

5. Is your home in the proper headship order—Lord Jesus, husband, wife, children? Is everyone functioning God's way in his or her role?

6. Is your home a place of security, protection, safety, and comfort for each member?

7. Does your home have boundaries? Do you need to set any new boundaries? Are they set in love?

8. If we took a portrait of your family right now, how would you evaluate the results?

Memory Verse

EPHESIANS 5:23–25—*"For the husband is the head of the wife, even as Christ is the head of the church: and he is the saviour of the body. Therefore as the church is subject unto Christ, so let the wives be to their own husbands in every thing. Husbands, love your wives, even as Christ also loved the church, and gave himself for it;"*

The Hidden Enemy of the Home

Key Verses

"Be ye angry, and sin not: let not the sun go down upon your wrath: Neither give place to the devil. Let him that stole steal no more: but rather let him labour, working with his hands the thing which is good, that he may have to give to him that needeth. Let no corrupt communication proceed out of your mouth, but that which is good to the use of edifying, that it may minister grace unto the hearers. And grieve not the holy Spirit of God, whereby ye are sealed unto the day of redemption. Let all bitterness, and wrath, and anger, and clamour, and evil speaking, be put away from you, with all malice: And be ye kind one to another, tenderhearted, forgiving one another, even as God for Christ's sake hath forgiven you."—EPHESIANS 4:26–32

Overview

Perhaps the most effective tool in Satan's arsenal against the home is unresolved anger. On the road to marital intimacy, there will be conflicts. The proper handling of those conflicts builds your confidence in each other and strengthens your marriage. The improper handling of conflicts breeds anger that undermines the marriage.

Introduction

_____

_____

_____

I. We Must _____ Anger

A. *Refuse To _____ Anger*
"Be ye angry, and sin not: let not the sun go down upon your wrath."—EPHESIANS 4:26

B. *Refuse To _____ Satan*
"Neither give place to the devil."—EPHESIANS 4:27

II. We Must _____ Anger

A. *Guard Your _____*
"And grieve not the holy Spirit of God, whereby ye are sealed unto the day of redemption."—EPHESIANS 4:30

B. *Guard Your _____*
"Let no corrupt communication proceed out of your mouth, but that which is good to the use of edifying, that it may minister grace unto the hearers."
—EPHESIANS 4:29

"Be not deceived: evil communications corrupt good manners."—1 Corinthians 15:33

"…Out of the abundance of the heart the mouth speaketh." —Matthew 12:34

III. We Must _____ Anger

A. Replace Anger with _____

B. Replace Anger with _____

"Forbearing one another, and forgiving one another, if any man have a quarrel against any: even as Christ forgave you, so also do ye."—Colossians 3:13

"And forgive us our debts, as we forgive our debtors." —Matthew 6:12

Conclusion

_____

_____

_____

Study Questions

1. What is Satan's most effective tool against the home?

2. What are the six primary internal causes of conflict in marriage?

3. List the ten ineffective responses to conflict. Are you practicing any of them?

4. List the seven steps of resolving conflict.

5. How could you apply these seven steps to a conflict you are facing right now?

6. Are you a pursuer or a withdrawer?

7. What two qualities replace anger?

8. Are you holding anything in your heart against your spouse right now?

Memory Verse

EPHESIANS 4:30—*"And grieve not the holy Spirit of God, whereby ye are sealed unto the day of redemption."*

Leaving a Godly Legacy

Key Verses

"Children, obey your parents in the Lord: for this is right. Honor thy father and mother; (which is the first commandment with promise;) That it may be well with thee, and thou mayest live long on the earth. And, ye fathers, provoke not your children to wrath: but bring them up in the nurture and admonition of the Lord."—EPHESIANS 6:1–4

Overview

The Bible says, *"Children are an heritage of the Lord"* —Psalm 127:3. The word *heritage* means "a possession or an inheritance." In other words, your children are precious gifts from God and you should view them as such. We have an opportunity and responsibility to rear them to follow and to love God with all their hearts.

Introduction

_____

_____

_____

I. _____ the Christian Life before Our Children

A. Model the Christian Life in Our _____ _____

"My son, give me thine heart, and let thine eyes observe my ways."—PROVERBS 23:26

"…Ye fathers, provoke not your children to wrath…."
—EPHESIANS 6:4

B. Model the Christian Life in Our _____

II. _____ our Children in the Christian Life

A. We Mentor Children by _____ *Them*

B. We Mentor Children by _____ _____ *with Them*

C. We Mentor Children by _____ *Them*

III. _____ Consistent Biblical Teaching

A. *Consistently Teach the Bible in the* _____

"My son, hear the instruction of thy father, and forsake not the law of thy mother:"—PROVERBS 1:8

1. TEACH THEM _____

2. TEACH THEM _____

3. TEACH THEM _____

B. *Consistently Teach the Bible in the* _____

Conclusion

_____

_____

_____

Study Questions

1. What is the greatest gift a father can give his children?

2. Not only do we need to model, we also need to
    _____.

3. What are three ways of mentoring your children?

4. Where are the two main places the Bible should be
    taught?

5. Is your husband/wife relationship reflecting Christ
    and the church?

6. How many times have you encouraged your wife or children through words today?

7. List some ways you can make the Scripture more visible in your home.

8. Will those who come behind you find you faithful?

Memory Verse

JOSHUA 24:15—*"And if it seem evil unto you to serve the LORD, choose you this day whom ye will serve; whether the gods which your fathers served that were on the other side of the flood, or the gods of the Amorites, in whose land ye dwell: but as for me and my house, we will serve the LORD."*

Striving Together
Publications

For additional Christian
growth resources visit
www.strivingtogether.com